Contents

Mental Health Medications

Medications are used to treat the symptoms of mental disorders such as schizophrenia, depression, bipolar disorder (sometimes called manic-depressive illness), anxiety disorders, and attention deficit-hyperactivity disorder (ADHD). Sometimes medications are used with other treatments such as psychotherapy. This guide describes:

- Types of medications used to treat mental disorders
- Side effects of medications
- Directions for taking medications
- Warnings about medications from the U.S. Food and Drug Administration (FDA).

This booklet does not provide information about diagnosing mental disorders. Choosing the right medication, medication dose, and treatment plan should be based on a person's individual needs and medical situation, and under a doctor's care.

Information about medications is frequently updated. Check the FDA website (http://www.fda.gov) for the latest information on warnings, patient medication guides, or newly approved medications. Throughout this document you will see two names for medications—the generic name and in parenthesis, the trade name. An example is fluoxetine (Prozac). See the end of this document for a complete alphabetical listing of medications.

What are psychiatric medications?

Psychiatric medications treat mental disorders. Sometimes called psychotropic or psychothera-peutic medications, they have changed the lives of people with mental disorders for the better. Many people with mental disorders live fulfilling lives with the help of these medications. Without them, people with mental disorders might suffer serious and disabling symptoms.

How are medications used to treat mental disorders?

Medications treat the symptoms of mental disorders. They cannot cure the disorder, but they make people feel better so they can function.

Medications work differently for different people. Some people get great results from medications and only need them for a short time. For example, a person with depression may feel much better after taking a medication for a few months, and may never need it again. People with disorders like schizophrenia or bipolar disorder, or people who have long-term or severe depression or anxiety may need to take medication for a much longer time.

Some people get side effects from medications and other people don't. Doses can be small or large, depending on the medication and the person. Factors that can affect how medications work in people include:

- Type of mental disorder, such as depression, anxiety, bipolar disorder, and schizophrenia
- Age, sex, and body size
- Physical illnesses
- Habits like smoking and drinking
- Liver and kidney function
- Genetics
- Other medications and herbal/vitamin supplements
- Diet
- Whether medications are taken as prescribed.

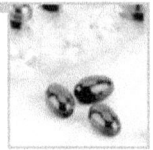

Antipsychotic medications are used to treat schizophrenia and schizophrenia-related disorders. Some of these medications have been available since the mid-1950's. They are also called conventional "typical" antipsychotics. Some of the more commonly used medications include:

- Chlorpromazine (Thorazine)
- Haloperidol (Haldol)
- Perphenazine (generic only)
- Fluphenazine (generic only).

In the 1990's, new antipsychotic medications were developed. These new medications are called second generation, or "atypical" antipsychotics.

One of these medications was clozapine (Clozaril). It is a very effective medication that treats psychotic symptoms, hallucinations, and breaks with reality, such as when a person believes he or she is the president. But clozapine can sometimes cause a serious problem called agranulocytosis, which is a loss of the white blood cells that help a person fight infection. Therefore, people who take clozapine must get their white blood cell counts checked every week or two. This problem and the cost of blood tests make treatment with clozapine difficult for many people. Still, clozapine is potentially helpful for people who do not respond to other antipsychotic medications.

Other atypical antipsychotics were developed. All of them are effective, and none cause agranulocytosis. These include:

- Risperidone (Risperdal)
- Olanzapine (Zyprexa)
- Quetiapine (Seroquel)
- Ziprasidone (Geodon)
- Aripiprazole (Abilify)
- Paliperidone (Invega).

The antipsychotics listed here are some of the medications used to treat symptoms of schizophrenia. Additional antipsychotics and other medications used for schizophrenia are listed in the chart at the end.

Note: The FDA issued a Public Health Advisory for atypical antipsychotic medications. The FDA determined that death rates are higher for elderly people with dementia when taking this medication. A review of data has found a risk with conventional antipsychotics as well. Antipsychotic medications are not FDA-approved for the treatment of behavioral disorders in patients with dementia.

What are the side effects?

Some people have side effects when they start taking these medications. Most side effects go away after a few days and often can be managed successfully. People who are taking antipsychotics should not drive until they adjust to their new medication. Side effects of many antipsychotics include:

- Drowsiness
- Dizziness when changing positions
- Blurred vision
- Rapid heartbeat
- Sensitivity to the sun
- Skin rashes
- Menstrual problems for women.

Atypical antipsychotic medications can cause major weight gain and changes in a person's metabolism. This may increase a person's risk of getting diabetes and high cholesterol.[1] A person's weight, glucose levels, and lipid levels should be monitored regularly by a doctor while taking an atypical antipsychotic medication.

Typical antipsychotic medications can cause side effects related to physical movement, such as:
- Rigidity
- Persistent muscle spasms
- Tremors
- Restlessness.

Long-term use of typical antipsychotic medications may lead to a condition called tardive dyskinesia (TD). TD causes muscle movements a person can't control. The movements commonly happen around the mouth. TD can range from mild to severe, and in some people the problem cannot be cured. Sometimes people with TD recover partially or fully after they stop taking the medication.

Every year, an estimated 5 percent of people taking typical antipsychotics get TD. The condition happens to fewer people who take the new, atypical antipsychotics, but some people may still get TD. People who think that they might have TD should check with their doctor before stopping their medication.

How are antipsychotics taken and how do people respond to them?

Antipsychotics are usually pills that people swallow, or liquid they can drink. Some antipsychotics are shots that are given once or twice a month.

Symptoms of schizophrenia, such as feeling agitated and having hallucinations, usually go away within days. Symptoms like delusions usually go away within a few weeks. After about six weeks, many people will see a lot of improvement.

However, people respond in different ways to antipsychotic medications, and no one can tell beforehand how a person will respond. Sometimes a person needs to try several medications before finding the right one. Doctors and patients can work together to find the best medication or medication combination, and dose.

Some people may have a relapse—their symptoms come back or get worse. Usually, relapses happen when people stop taking their medication, or when they only take it sometimes. Some people stop taking the medication because they feel better or they may feel they don't need it anymore. **But no one should stop taking an antipsychotic medication without talking to his or her doctor.** When a doctor says it is okay to stop taking a medication, it should be gradually tapered off, never stopped suddenly.

How do antipsychotics interact with other medications?

Antipsychotics can produce unpleasant or dangerous side effects when taken with certain medications. For this reason, all doctors treating a patient need to be aware of all the medications that person is taking. Doctors need to know about prescription and over-the-counter medicine, vitamins, minerals, and herbal supplements. People also need to discuss any alcohol or other drug use with their doctor.

To find out more about how antipsychotics work, the National Institute of Mental Health (NIMH) funded a study called CATIE (Clinical Antipsychotic Trials of Intervention Effectiveness). This study compared the effectiveness and side effects of five antipsychotics used to treat people with schizophrenia. In general, the study found that the older medication perphenazine worked as well as the newer, atypical medications. But because people respond differently to different medications, it is important that treatments be designed carefully for each person. You can find more information at http:// www.nimh.nih.gov/trials/practical/catie/index.shtml.

What medications are used to treat depression?

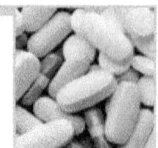

Depression is commonly treated with antidepressant medications. Antidepressants work to balance some of the natural chemicals in our brains. These chemicals are called neurotransmitters, and they affect our mood and emotional responses. Antidepressants work on neurotransmitters such as serotonin, norepinephrine, and dopamine.

The most popular types of antidepressants are called selective serotonin reuptake inhibitors (SSRIs). These include:

- Fluoxetine (Prozac)
- Citalopram (Celexa)
- Sertraline (Zoloft)
- Paroxetine (Paxil)
- Escitalopram (Lexapro).

Other types of antidepressants are serotonin and norepinephrine reuptake inhibitors (SNRIs). SNRIs are similar to SSRIs and include venlafaxine (Effexor) and duloxetine (Cymbalta). Another antidepressant that is commonly used is bupropion (Wellbutrin). Bupropion, which works on the neurotransmitter dopamine, is unique in that it does not fit into any specific drug type.

SSRIs and SNRIs are popular because they do not cause as many side effects as older classes of antidepressants. Older antidepressant medications include tricyclics, tetracyclics, and monoamine oxidase inhibitors (MAOIs). For some people, tricyclics, tetracyclics, or MAOIs may be the best medications.

What are the side effects?

Antidepressants may cause mild side effects that usually do not last long. **Any unusual reactions or side effects should be reported to a doctor immediately.**

The most common side effects associated with SSRIs and SNRIs include:

- Headache, which usually goes away within a few days.
- Nausea (feeling sick to your stomach), which usually goes away within a few days.
- Sleeplessness or drowsiness, which may happen during the first few weeks but then goes away. Sometimes the medication dose needs to be reduced or the time of day it is taken needs to be adjusted to help lessen these side effects.
- Agitation (feeling jittery).
- Sexual problems, which can affect both men and women and may include reduced sex drive, and problems having and enjoying sex.

Tricyclic antidepressants can cause side effects, including:

- Dry mouth.
- Constipation.
- Bladder problems. It may be hard to empty the bladder, or the urine stream may not be as strong as usual. Older men with enlarged prostate conditions may be more affected.
- Sexual problems, which can affect both men and women and may include reduced sex drive, and problems having and enjoying sex.

- Blurred vision, which usually goes away quickly.
- Drowsiness. Usually, antidepressants that make you drowsy are taken at bedtime.

People taking MAOIs need to be careful about the foods they eat and the medicines they take. Foods and medicines that contain high levels of a chemical called tyramine are dangerous for people taking MAOIs. Tyramine is found in some cheeses, wines, and pickles. The chemical is also in some medications, including decongestants and over-the-counter cold medicine.

Mixing MAOIs and tyramine can cause a sharp increase in blood pressure, which can lead to stroke. People taking MAOIs should ask their doctors for a complete list of foods, medicines, and other substances to avoid. An MAOI skin patch has recently been developed and may help reduce some of these risks. A doctor can help a person figure out if a patch or a pill will work for him or her.

How should antidepressants be taken?

People taking antidepressants need to follow their doctors' directions. The medication should be taken in the right dose for the right amount of time. It can take three or four weeks until the medicine takes effect. Some people take the medications for a short time, and some people take them for much longer periods. People with long-term or severe depression may need to take medication for a long time.

Once a person is taking antidepressants, it is important not to stop taking them without the help of a doctor. Sometimes people taking antidepressants feel better and stop taking the medication too soon, and the depression may return. When it is time to stop the medication, the doctor will help the person slowly and safely decrease the dose. It's important to give the body

time to adjust to the change. People don't get addicted, or "hooked," on the medications, but stopping them abruptly can cause withdrawal symptoms.

If a medication does not work, it is helpful to be open to trying another one. A study funded by NIMH found that if a person with difficult-to-treat depression did not get better with a first medication, chances of getting better increased when the person tried a new one or added a second medication to his or her treatment. The study was called STAR*D (Sequenced Treatment Alternatives to Relieve Depression).[2,3] For more information, visit http://www.nimh.nih.gov/trials/practical/stard/index.shtml.

Are herbal medicines used to treat depression?

The herbal medicine St. John's wort has been used for centuries in many folk and herbal remedies. Today in Europe, it is used widely to treat mild-to-moderate depression. In the United States, it is one of the top-selling botanical products.

The National Institutes of Health conducted a clinical trial to determine the effectiveness of treating adults who have major depression with St. Johns wort. The study included 340 people diagnosed with major depression. One-third of the people took the herbal medicine, one-third took an SSRI, and one-third took a placebo, or "sugar pill." The people did not know what they were taking. The study found that St. John's wort was no more effective than the placebo in treating major depression.[4] A study currently in progress is looking at the effectiveness of St. John's wort for treating mild or minor depression.

Other research has shown that St. John's wort can dangerously interact with other medications, including those used to control HIV. On February

10, 2000, the FDA issued a Public Health Advisory letter stating that the herb appears to interfere with certain medications used to treat heart disease, depression, seizures, certain cancers, and organ transplant rejection. Also, St. Johns wort may interfere with oral contraceptives.

Because St. John's wort may not mix well with other medications, people should always talk with their doctors before taking it or any herbal supplement.

FDA warning on antidepressants

Antidepressants are safe and popular, but some studies have suggested that they may have unintentional effects, especially in young people. In 2004, the FDA looked at published and unpublished data on trials of antidepressants that involved nearly 4,400 children and adolescents. They found that 4 percent of those taking antidepressants thought about or tried suicide (although no suicides occurred), compared to 2 percent of those receiving placebos (sugar pill).

In 2005, the FDA decided to adopt a "black box" warning label—the most serious type of warning— on all antidepressant medications. The warning says there is an increased risk of suicidal thinking or attempts in children and adolescents taking antidepressants. In 2007, the FDA proposed that makers of all antidepressant medications extend the warning to include young adults up through age 24.

The warning also says that patients of all ages taking antidepressants should be watched closely, especially during the first few weeks of treatment. Possible side effects to look for are depression that gets worse, suicidal thinking or behavior, or any unusual changes in behavior such as trouble sleeping, agitation, or withdrawal from normal social situations. Families and caregivers should report any changes to the doctor. The latest information from the FDA can be found at http://www.fda.gov.

Results of a comprehensive review of pediatric trials conducted between 1988 and 2006 suggested that the benefits of antidepressant medications likely outweigh their risks to children and adolescents with major depression and anxiety disorders.[5] The study was funded in part by NIMH.

Finally, the FDA has warned that combining the newer SSRI or SNRI antidepressants with one of the commonly-used "triptan" medications used to treat migraine headaches could cause a life-threatening illness called "serotonin syndrome." A person with serotonin syndrome may be agitated, have hallucinations (see or hear things that are not real), have a high temperature, or have unusual blood pressure changes. Serotonin syndrome is usually associated with the older antidepressants called MAOIs, but it can happen with the newer antidepressants as well, if they are mixed with the wrong medications.

What medications are used to treat bipolar disorder?

Bipolar disorder, also called manic-depressive illness, is commonly treated with mood stabilizers. Sometimes, antipsychotics and antidepressants are used along with a mood stabilizer.

Mood stabilizers

People with bipolar disorder usually try mood stabilizers first. In general, people continue treatment with mood stabilizers for years. Lithium is a very effective mood stabilizer. It was the first mood stabilizer approved by the FDA in the 1970's for treating both manic and depressive episodes.

Anticonvulsant medications also are used as mood stabilizers. They were originally developed to treat seizures, but they were found to help control moods as well. One anticonvulsant commonly used as a mood stabilizer is valproic acid, also called divalproex sodium (Depakote). For some people, it may work better than lithium.[6] Other anticonvulsants used as mood stabilizers are carbamazepine (Tegretol), lamotrigine (Lamictal) and oxcarbazepine (Trileptal).

Atypical antipsychotics

Atypical antipsychotic medications are sometimes used to treat symptoms of bipolar disorder. Often, antipsychotics are used along with other medications.

Antipsychotics used to treat people with bipolar disorder include:

- Olanzapine (Zyprexa), which helps people with severe or psychotic depression, which often is accompanied by a break with reality, hallucinations, or delusions[7]
- Aripiprazole (Abilify), which can be taken as a pill or as a shot
- Risperidone (Risperdal)
- Ziprasidone (Geodon)
- Clozapine (Clorazil), which is often used for people who do not respond to lithium or anticonvulsants.[8]

Antidepressants

Antidepressants are sometimes used to treat symptoms of depression in bipolar disorder. Fluoxetine (Prozac), paroxetine (Paxil), or sertraline (Zoloft) are a few that are used. However, people with bipolar disorder should not take an antidepressant on its own. Doing so can cause the person to rapidly switch from depression to mania, which can be dangerous.[9] To prevent this problem, doctors give patients a mood stabilizer or an antipsychotic along with an antidepressant.

Research on whether antidepressants help people with bipolar depression is mixed. An NIMH-funded study found that antidepressants were no more effective than a placebo to help treat depression in people with bipolar disorder. The people were taking mood stabilizers along with the antidepressants. You can find out more about this study, called STEP-BD (Systematic Treatment Enhancement Program for Bipolar Disorder),[10] at http://www.nimh.nih.gov/trials/practical/step-bd/index.shtml.

What are the side effects?

Treatments for bipolar disorder have improved over the last 10 years. But everyone responds differently to medications. If you have any side effects, tell your doctor right away. He or she may change the dose or prescribe a different medication.

Different medications for treating bipolar disorder may cause different side effects. Some medications used for treating bipolar disorder have been linked to unique and serious symptoms, which are described below.

Lithium can cause several side effects, and some of them may become serious. They include:
- Loss of coordination
- Excessive thirst
- Frequent urination
- Blackouts
- Seizures
- Slurred speech
- Fast, slow, irregular, or pounding heartbeat
- Hallucinations (seeing things or hearing voices that do not exist)
- Changes in vision
- Itching, rash
- Swelling of the eyes, face, lips, tongue, throat, hands, feet, ankles, or lower legs.

If a person with bipolar disorder is being treated with lithium, he or she should visit the doctor regularly to check the levels of lithium in the blood, and make sure the kidneys and the thyroid are working normally.

Some possible side effects linked with valproic acid/divalproex sodium include:
- Changes in weight
- Nausea
- Stomach pain
- Vomiting
- Anorexia
- Loss of appetite.

Valproic acid may cause damage to the liver or pancreas, so people taking it should see their doctors regularly.

Valproic acid may affect young girls and women in unique ways. Sometimes, valproic acid may increase testosterone (a male hormone) levels in teenage girls and lead to a condition called polycystic ovarian syndrome (PCOS).[11,12] PCOS is a disease that can affect fertility and make the menstrual cycle become irregular, but symptoms tend to go away after valproic acid is stopped.[13] It also may cause birth defects in women who are pregnant.

Lamotrigine can cause a rare but serious skin rash that needs to be treated in a hospital. In some cases, this rash can cause permanent disability or be life-threatening.

In addition, valproic acid, lamotrigine, carbamazepine, oxcarbazepine and other anticonvulsant medications (listed in the chart at the end of this document) have an FDA warning. The warning states that their use may increase the risk of suicidal thoughts and behaviors. People taking anticonvulsant medications for bipolar or other illnesses should be closely monitored for new or worsening symptoms of depression, suicidal thoughts or behavior, or any unusual changes in mood or behavior. People taking these medications should not make any changes without talking to their health care professional.

Other medications for bipolar disorder may also be linked with rare but serious side effects. Always talk with the doctor or pharmacist about any potential side effects before taking the medication.

For information on side effects of antipsychotics, see the section on medications for treating schizophrenia.

For information on side effects and FDA warnings of antidepressants, see the section on medications for treating depression.

How should medications for bipolar disorder be taken?

Medications should be taken as directed by a doctor. Sometimes a person's treatment plan needs to be changed. When changes in medicine are needed, the doctor will guide the change. **A person should never stop taking a medication without asking a doctor for help.**

There is no cure for bipolar disorder, but treatment works for many people. Treatment works best when it is continuous, rather than on and off. However, mood changes can happen even when there are no breaks in treatment. Patients should be open with their doctors about treatment. Talking about how treatment is working can help it be more effective.

It may be helpful for people or their family members to keep a daily chart of mood symptoms, treatments, sleep patterns, and life events. This chart can help patients and doctors track the illness. Doctors can use the chart to treat the illness most effectively.

Because medications for bipolar disorder can have serious side effects, it is important for anyone taking them to see the doctor regularly to check for possibly dangerous changes in the body.

What medications are used to treat anxiety disorders?

Antidepressants, anti-anxiety medications, and beta-blockers are the most common medications used for anxiety disorders.

Anxiety disorders include:

- Obsessive compulsive disorder (OCD)
- Post-traumatic stress disorder (PTSD)
- Generalized anxiety disorder (GAD)
- Panic disorder
- Social phobia.

Antidepressants

Antidepressants were developed to treat depression, but they also help people with anxiety disorders. SSRIs such as fluoxetine (Prozac), sertraline (Zoloft), escitalopram (Lexapro), paroxetine (Paxil), and citalopram (Celexa) are commonly prescribed for panic disorder, OCD, PTSD, and social phobia. The SNRI venlafaxine (Effexor) is commonly used to treat GAD. The antidepressant bupropion (Wellbutrin) is also sometimes used. When treating anxiety disorders, antidepressants generally are started at low doses and increased over time.

Some tricyclic antidepressants work well for anxiety. For example, imipramine (Tofranil) is prescribed for panic disorder and GAD. Clomipramine (Anafranil) is used to treat OCD. Tricyclics are also started at low doses and increased over time.

MAOIs are also used for anxiety disorders. Doctors sometimes prescribe phenelzine (Nardil), tranylcypromine (Parnate), and isocarboxazid (Marplan). People who take MAOIs must avoid certain food and medicines that can interact with their medicine and cause dangerous increases in blood pressure. For more information, see the section on medications used to treat depression.

Benzodiazepines (anti-anxiety medications)

The anti-anxiety medications called benzodiazepines can start working more quickly than antidepressants. The ones used to treat anxiety disorders include:

- Clonazepam (Klonopin), which is used for social phobia and GAD
- Lorazepam (Ativan), which is used for panic disorder
- Alprazolam (Xanax), which is used for panic disorder and GAD.

Buspirone (Buspar) is an anti-anxiety medication used to treat GAD. Unlike benzodiazepines, however, it takes at least two weeks for buspirone to begin working.

Clonazepam, listed above, is an anticonvulsant medication. See FDA warning on anticonvulsants under the bipolar disorder section.

Beta-blockers

Beta-blockers control some of the physical symptoms of anxiety, such as trembling and sweating. Propranolol (Inderal) is a beta-blocker usually used to treat heart conditions and high blood pressure. The medicine also helps people who have physical problems related to anxiety. For example, when a person with social phobia must face a stressful situation, such as giving a speech, or attending an important meeting, a doctor may prescribe a beta-blocker. Taking the medicine for a short period of time can help the person keep physical symptoms under control.

What are the side effects?

See the section on antidepressants for a discussion on side effects.

The most common side effects for benzodiazepines are drowsiness and dizziness. Other possible side effects include:

- Upset stomach
- Blurred vision
- Headache
- Confusion
- Grogginess
- Nightmares.

Possible side effects from buspirone (BuSpar) include:

- Dizziness
- Headaches
- Nausea
- Nervousness
- Lightheadedness
- Excitement
- Trouble sleeping.

Common side effects from beta-blockers include:

- Fatigue
- Cold hands
- Dizziness
- Weakness.

In addition, beta-blockers generally are not recommended for people with asthma or diabetes because they may worsen symptoms.

How should medications for anxiety disorders be taken?

People can build a tolerance to benzodiazepines if they are taken over a long period of time and may need higher and higher doses to get the same effect. Some people may become dependent on them. To avoid these problems, doctors usually prescribe the medication for short periods, a practice that is especially helpful for people who have substance abuse problems or who become dependent on medication easily. If people suddenly stop taking benzodiazepines, they may get withdrawal symptoms, or their anxiety may return. Therefore, they should be tapered off slowly.

Buspirone and beta-blockers are similar. They are usually taken on a short-term basis for anxiety. Both should be tapered off slowly. Talk to the doctor before stopping any anti-anxiety medication.

Attention deficit/hyperactivity disorder (ADHD) occurs in both children and adults. ADHD is commonly treated with stimulants, such as:

- Methylphenidate (Ritalin, Metadate, Concerta, Daytrana)
- Amphetamine (Adderall)
- Dextroamphetamine (Dexedrine, Dextrostat).

In 2002, the FDA approved the nonstimulant medication atomoxetine (Strattera) for use as a treatment for ADHD. In February 2007, the FDA approved the use of the stimulant lisdexamfetamine dimesylate (Vyvanse) for the treatment of ADHD in children ages 6 to 12 years.

What are the side effects?

Most side effects are minor and disappear when dosage levels are lowered. The most common side effects include:

- Decreased appetite. Children seem to be less hungry during the middle of the day, but they are often hungry by dinnertime as the medication wears off.
- Sleep problems. If a child cannot fall asleep, the doctor may prescribe a lower dose. The doctor might also suggest that parents give the medication to their child earlier in the day, or stop the afternoon or evening dose. To help ease sleeping problems, a doctor may add a prescription for a low dose of an antidepressant or a medication called clonidine.

- Stomachaches and headaches.
- **Less common side effects.** A few children develop sudden, repetitive movements or sounds called tics. These tics may or may not be noticeable. Changing the medication dosage may make tics go away. Some children also may appear to have a personality change, such as appearing "flat" or without emotion. Talk with your child's doctor if you see any of these side effects.

How are ADHD medications taken?

Stimulant medications can be short-acting or long-acting, and can be taken in different forms such as a pill, patch, or powder. Long-acting, sustained and extended release forms allow children to take the medication just once a day before school. Parents and doctors should decide together which medication is best for the child and whether the child needs medication only for school hours or for evenings and weekends too.

ADHD medications help many children and adults who are hyperactive and impulsive. They help people focus, work, and learn. Stimulant medication also may improve physical coordination. However, different people respond differently to medications, so children taking ADHD medications should be watched closely.

Are ADHD medications safe?

Stimulant medications are safe when given under a doctor's supervision. Some children taking them may feel slightly different or "funny."

Some parents worry that stimulant medications may lead to drug abuse or dependence, but there is little evidence of this. Research shows that teens with ADHD who took stimulant medications were less likely to abuse drugs than those who did not take stimulant medications.[14]

FDA warning on possible rare side effects

In 2007, the FDA required that all makers of ADHD medications develop Patient Medication Guides. The guides must alert patients to possible heart and psychiatric problems related to ADHD medicine. The FDA required the Patient Medication Guides because a review of data found that ADHD patients with heart conditions had a slightly higher risk of strokes, heart attacks, and sudden death when taking the medications. The review also found a slightly higher risk (about 1 in 1,000) for medication-related psychiatric problems, such as hearing voices, having hallucinations, becoming suspicious for no reason, or becoming manic. This happened to patients who had no history of psychiatric problems.

The FDA recommends that any treatment plan for ADHD include an initial health and family history examination. This exam should look for existing heart and psychiatric problems.

The non-stimulant ADHD medication called atomoxetine (Strattera) carries another warning. Studies show that children and teenagers with ADHD who take atomoxetine are more likely to have suicidal thoughts than children and teenagers with ADHD who do not take atomoxetine. If your child is taking atomoxetine, watch his or her behavior carefully. A child may develop serious symptoms suddenly, so it is important to pay attention to your child's behavior every day. Ask other people who spend a lot of time with your child, such as brothers, sisters, and teachers, to tell you if they notice changes in your child's behavior. Call a doctor right away if your child shows any of the following symptoms:

- Acting more subdued or withdrawn than usual
- Feeling helpless, hopeless, or worthless
- New or worsening depression
- Thinking or talking about hurting himself or herself
- Extreme worry
- Agitation
- Panic attacks
- Trouble sleeping
- Irritability
- Aggressive or violent behavior
- Acting without thinking
- Extreme increase in activity or talking
- Frenzied, abnormal excitement
- Any sudden or unusual changes in behavior.

While taking atomoxetine, your child should see a doctor often, especially at the beginning of treatment. Be sure that your child keeps all appointments with his or her doctor.

Which groups have special needs when taking psychiatric medications?

Psychiatric medications are taken by all types of people, but some groups have special needs, including:

- Children and adolescents
- Older adults
- Women who are pregnant or may become pregnant.

Children and adolescents

Most medications used to treat young people with mental illness are safe and effective. However, many medications have not been studied or approved for use with children. Researchers are not sure how these medications affect a child's growing body. Still, a doctor can give a young person an FDA-approved medication on an "off-label" basis. This means that the doctor prescribes the medication to help the patient even though the medicine is not approved for the specific mental disorder or age.

For these reasons, it is important to watch young people who take these medications. Young people may have different reactions and side effects than adults. Also, some medications, including antidepressants and ADHD medications, carry FDA warnings about potentially dangerous side effects for young people. See the sections on antidepressants and ADHD medications for more information about these warnings.

More research is needed on how these medications affect children and adolescents. NIMH has funded studies on this topic. For example, NIMH funded the Preschoolers with ADHD Treatment Study (PATS), which involved 300 preschoolers (3 to 5 years old) diagnosed with ADHD. The study found that low doses of the stimulant methylphenidate are safe and effective for preschoolers. However, children of this age are more sensitive to the side effects of the medication, including slower growth rates. Children taking methylphenidate should be watched closely.[15,16,17]

In addition to medications, other treatments for young people with mental disorders should be considered. Psychotherapy, family therapy, educational courses, and behavior management techniques can help everyone involved cope with the disorder. For more information on child and adolescent mental health research, visit http://www. nimh.nih.gov/health/topics/child-and-adolescent-mental-health/index.shtml.

Older adults

Because older people often have more medical problems than other groups, they tend to take more medications than younger people, including prescribed, over-the-counter, and herbal medications. As a result, older people have a higher risk for experiencing bad drug interactions, missing doses, or overdosing.

Older people also tend to be more sensitive to medications. Even healthy older people react to medications differently than younger people because their bodies process it more slowly. Therefore, lower or less frequent doses may be needed.

Sometimes memory problems affect older people who take medications for mental disorders. An older adult may forget his or her regular dose and take too much or not enough. A good way to keep track of medicine is to use a seven-day pill box, which can be bought at any pharmacy. At the beginning of each week, older adults and their caregivers fill the box so that it is easy to remember what medicine to take. Many pharmacies also have pillboxes with sections for medications that must be taken more than once a day.

Women who are pregnant or may become pregnant

The research on the use of psychiatric medications during pregnancy is limited. The risks are different depending on what medication is taken, and at what point during the pregnancy the medication is taken.

Research has shown that antidepressants, especially SSRIs, are safe during pregnancy. Birth defects or other problems are possible, but they are very rare.[18,19]

However, antidepressant medications do cross the placental barrier and may reach the fetus. Some research suggests the use of SSRIs during pregnancy is associated with miscarriage or birth defects, but other studies do not support this.[20] Studies have also found that fetuses exposed to SSRIs during the third trimester may be born with "withdrawal" symptoms such as breathing problems, jitteriness, irritability, trouble feeding, or hypoglycemia (low blood sugar).

Most studies have found that these symptoms in babies are generally mild and short-lived, and no deaths have been reported. On the flip side, women who stop taking their antidepressant medication during pregnancy may get depression again and may put both themselves and their infant at risk.[20,21]

In 2004, the FDA issued a warning against the use of certain antidepressants in the late third trimester. The warning said that doctors may want to gradually taper pregnant women off antidepressants in the third trimester so that the baby is not affected.[22] After a woman delivers, she should consult with her doctor to decide whether to return to a full dose during the period when she is most vulnerable to postpartum depression.

Some medications should not be taken during pregnancy. Benzodiazepines may cause birth defects or other infant problems, especially if taken during the first trimester. Mood stabilizers are known to cause birth defects. Benzodiazepines and lithium have been shown to cause "floppy baby syndrome," which is when a baby is drowsy and limp, and cannot breathe or feed well.

Research suggests that taking antipsychotic medications during pregnancy can lead to birth defects, especially if they are taken during the first trimester. But results vary widely depending on the type of antipsychotic. The conventional antipsychotic haloperidol has been studied more than others, and has been found not to cause birth defects.[23,24]

After the baby is born, women and their doctors should watch for postpartum depression, especially if they stopped taking their medication during pregnancy. In addition, women who nurse while taking psychiatric medications should know that a small amount of the medication passes into the breast milk. However, the medication may or may not affect the baby. It depends on the medication and when it is taken. Women taking psychiatric medications and who intend to breastfeed should discuss the potential risks and benefits with their doctors.

Decisions on medication should be based on each woman's needs and circumstances. Medications should be selected based on available scientific research, and they should be taken at the lowest possible dose. Pregnant women should be watched closely throughout their pregnancy and after delivery.

What should I ask my doctor if I am prescribed a psychiatric medication?

You and your family can help your doctor find the right medications for you. The doctor needs to know your medical history; family history; information about allergies; other medications, supplements or herbal remedies you take; and other details about your overall health. You or a family member should ask the following questions when a medication is prescribed:

- What is the name of the medication?
- What is the medication supposed to do?
- How and when should I take it?
- How much should I take?
- What should I do if I miss a dose?
- When and how should I stop taking it?
- Will it interact with other medications I take?
- Do I need to avoid any types of food or drink while taking the medication? What should I avoid?
- Should it be taken with or without food?
- Is it safe to drink alcohol while taking this medication?
- What are the side effects? What should I do if I experience them?
- Is the Patient Package Insert for the medication available?

After taking the medication for a short time, tell your doctor how you feel, if you are having side effects, and any concerns you have about the medicine.

Alphabetical List of Medications

This section identifies antipsychotic medications, antidepressant medications, mood stabilizers, anticonvulsant medications, anti-anxiety medications, and ADHD medications. Some medications are marketed under trade names, not all of which can be listed in this publication.

The first chart lists the medications by trade name; the second chart lists the medications by generic name. If your medication does not appear in this section, refer to the FDA website (http://www.fda.gov). Also, ask your doctor or pharmacist for more information about any medication.

Medications Organized by Trade Name

Trade Name	Generic Name	FDA Approved Age
Combination Antipsychotic and Antidepressant Medication		
Symbyax (Prozac & Zyprexa)	fluoxetine & olanzapine	18 and older
Antipsychotic Medications		
Abilify	aripiprazole	10 and older for bipolar disorder, manic, or mixed episodes; 13 to 17 for schizophrenia and bipolar
Clozaril	clozapine	18 and older
Fanapt	iloperidone	18 and older
fluphenazine (generic only)	fluphenazine	18 and older
Geodon	ziprasidone	18 and older
Haldol	haloperidol	3 and older
Invega	paliperidone	18 and older
Loxitane	loxapine	18 and older
Moban	molindone	18 and older
Navane	thiothixene	18 and older
Orap (for Tourette's syndrome)	pimozide	12 and older
perphenazine (generic only)	perphenazine	18 and older
Risperdal	risperidone	13 and older for schizophrenia; 10 and older for bipolar mania and mixed episodes; 5 to 16 for irritability associated with autism
Seroquel	quetiapine	13 and older for schizophrenia; 18 and older for bipolar; 10 to 17 for treatment of manic and mixed episodes of bipolar disorder
Stelazine	trifluoperazine	18 and older
thioridazine (generic only)	thioridazine	2 and older
Thorazine	chlorpromazine	18 and older
Zyprexa	olanzapine	18 and older; ages 13 to 17 as second line treatment for manic or mixed episodes of bipolar disorder and schizophrenia

Trade Name	Generic Name	FDA Approved Age
Antidepressant Medications (also used for anxiety disorders)		
Anafranil (tricyclic)	clomipramine	10 and older (for OCD only)
Asendin	amoxapine	18 and older
Aventyl (tricyclic)	nortriptyline	18 and older
Celexa (SSRI)	citalopram	18 and older
Cymbalta (SNRI)	duloxetine	18 and older
Desyrel	trazodone	18 and older
Effexor (SNRI)	venlafaxine	18 and older
Elavil (tricyclic)	amitriptyline	18 and older
Emsam	selegiline	18 and older
Lexapro (SSRI)	escitalopram	18 and older; 12 to 17 (for major depressive disorder)
Ludiomil (tricyclic)	maprotiline	18 and older
Luvox (SSRI)	fluvoxamine	8 and older (for OCD only)
Marplan (MAOI)	isocarboxazid	18 and older
Nardil (MAOI)	phenelzine	18 and older
Norpramin (tricyclic)	desipramine	18 and older
Pamelor (tricyclic)	nortriptyline	18 and older
Parnate (MAOI)	tranylcypromine	18 and older
Paxil (SSRI)	paroxetine	18 and older
Pexeva (SSRI)	paroxetine-mesylate	18 and older
Pristiq (SNRI)	desvenlafaxine	18 and older
Prozac (SSRI)	fluoxetine	8 and older
Remeron	mirtazapine	18 and older
Sarafem (SSRI)	fluoxetine	18 and older for premenstrual dysphoric disorder (PMDD)
Sinequan (tricyclic)	doxepin	12 and older
Surmontil (tricyclic)	trimipramine	18 and older
Tofranil (tricyclic)	imipramine	6 and older (for bedwetting)
Tofranil-PM (tricyclic)	imipramine pamoate	18 and older
Vivactil (tricyclic)	protriptyline	18 and older
Wellbutrin	bupropion	18 and older
Zoloft (SSRI)	sertraline	6 and older (for OCD only)

Trade Name	Generic Name	FDA Approved Age

Mood Stabilizing and Anticonvulsant Medications

Trade Name	Generic Name	FDA Approved Age
Depakote	divalproex sodium (valproic acid)	2 and older (for seizures)
Eskalith	lithium carbonate	12 and older
Lamictal	lamotrigine	18 and older
lithium citrate (generic only)	lithium citrate	12 and older
Lithobid	lithium carbonate	12 and older
Neurontin	gabapentin	18 and older
Tegretol	carbamazepine	any age (for seizures)
Topamax	topiramate	18 and older
Trileptal	oxcarbazepine	4 and older

Anti-anxiety Medications

(All of these anti-anxiety medications are benzodiazepines, except BuSpar)

Trade Name	Generic Name	FDA Approved Age
Ativan	lorazepam	18 and older
BuSpar	buspirone	18 and older
Klonopin	clonazepam	18 and older
Librium	chlordiazepoxide	18 and older
oxazepam (generic only)	oxazepam	18 and older
Tranxene	clorazepate	18 and older
Valium	diazepam	18 and older
Xanax	alprazolam	18 and older

Trade Name	Generic Name	FDA Approved Age

ADHD Medications

(All of these ADHD medications are stimulants, except Intuniv and Straterra.)

Trade Name	Generic Name	FDA Approved Age
Adderall	amphetamine	3 and older
Adderall XR	amphetamine (extended release)	6 and older
Concerta	methylphenidate (long acting)	6 and older
Daytrana	methylphenidate patch	6 and older
Desoxyn	methamphetamine	6 and older
Dexedrine	dextroamphetamine	3 and older
Dextrostat	dextroamphetamine	3 and older
Focalin	dexmethylphenidate	6 and older
Focalin XR	dexmethylphenidate (extended release)	6 and older
Intuniv	guanfacine	6 and older
Metadate ER	methylphenidate (extended release)	6 and older
Metadate CD	methylphenidate (extended release)	6 and older
Methylin	methylphenidate (oral solution and chewable tablets)	6 and older
Ritalin	methylphenidate	6 and older
Ritalin SR	methylphenidate (extended release)	6 and older
Ritalin LA	methylphenidate (long-acting)	6 and older
Strattera	atomoxetine	6 and older
Vyvanse	lisdexamfetamine dimesylate	6 and older

National Institute of Mental Health

Medications Organized by Generic Name

Generic Name	Trade Name	FDA Approved Age
Combination Antipsychotic and Antidepressant Medication		
fluoxetine & olanzapine	Symbyax (Prozac & Zyprexa)	18 and older
Antipsychotic Medications		
aripiprazole	Abilify	10 and older for bipolar disorder, manic, or mixed episodes; 13 to 17 for schizophrenia and bipolar
chlorpromazine	Thorazine	18 and older
clozapine	Clozaril	18 and older
fluphenazine (generic only)	fluphenazine	18 and older
haloperidol	Haldol	3 and older
iloperidone	Fanapt	18 and older
loxapine	Loxitane	18 and older
molindone	Moban	18 and older
olanzapine	Zyprexa	18 and older; ages 13 to 17 as second line treatment for manic or mixed episodes of bipolar disorder and schizophrenia
paliperidone	Invega	18 and older
perphenazine (generic only)	perphenazine	18 and older
pimozide (for Tourette's syndrome)	Orap	12 and older
quetiapine	Seroquel	13 and older for schizophrenia; 18 and older for bipolar; 10 to 17 for treatment of manic and mixed episodes of bipolar disorder
risperidone	Risperdal	13 and older for schizophrenia; 10 and older for bipolar mania and mixed episodes; 5 to 16 for irritability associated with autism
thioridazine (generic only)	thioridazine	2 and older
thiothixene	Navane	18 and older
trifluoperazine	Stelazine	18 and older
ziprasidone	Geodon	18 and older

Generic Name	Trade Name	FDA Approved Age
Antidepressant Medications (also used for anxiety disorders)		
amitriptyline (tricyclic)	Elavil	18 and older
amoxapine	Asendin	18 and older
bupropion	Wellbutrin	18 and older
citalopram (SSRI)	Celexa	18 and older
clomipramine (tricyclic)	Anafranil	10 and older (for OCD only)
desipramine (tricyclic)	Norpramin	18 and older
desvenlafaxine (SNRI)	Pristiq	18 and older
doxepin (tricyclic)	Sinequan	12 and older
duloxetine (SNRI)	Cymbalta	18 and older
escitalopram (SSRI)	Lexapro	18 and older; 12 to 17 (for major depressive disorder)
fluoxetine (SSRI)	Prozac	8 and older
fluoxetine (SSRI)	Sarafem	18 and older for premenstrual dysphoric disorder (PMDD)
fluvoxamine (SSRI)	Luvox	8 and older (for OCD only)
imipramine (tricyclic)	Tofranil	6 and older (for bedwetting)
imipramine pamoate (tricyclic)	Tofranil-PM	18 and older
isocarboxazid (MAOI)	Marplan	18 and older
maprotiline (tricyclic)	Ludiomil	18 and older
mirtazapine	Remeron	18 and older
nortriptyline (tricyclic)	Aventyl, Pamelor	18 and older
paroxetine (SSRI)	Paxil	18 and older
paroxetine mesylate (SSRI)	Pexeva	18 and older
phenelzine (MAOI)	Nardil	18 and older
protriptyline (tricyclic)	Vivactil	18 and older
selegiline	Emsam	18 and older
sertraline (SSRI)	Zoloft	6 and older (for OCD only)
tranylcypromine (MAOI)	Parnate	18 and older
trazodone	Desyrel	18 and older
trimipramine (tricyclic)	Surmontil	18 and older
venlafaxine (SNRI)	Effexor	18 and older

National Institute of Mental Health

Generic Name	Trade Name	FDA Approved Age

Mood Stabilizing and Anticonvulsant Medications

Generic Name	Trade Name	FDA Approved Age
carbamazepine	Tegretol	any age (for seizures)
divalproex sodium (valproic acid)	Depakote	2 and older (for seizures)
gabapentin	Neurontin	18 and older
lamotrigine	Lamictal	18 and older
lithium carbonate	Eskalith, Lithobid	12 and older
lithium citrate (generic only)	lithium citrate	12 and older
oxcarbazepine	Trileptal	4 and older
topiramate	Topamax	18 and older

Anti-anxiety Medications

(All of these anti-anxiety medications are benzodiazepines, except buspirone.)

Generic Name	Trade Name	FDA Approved Age
alprazolam	Xanax	18 and older
buspirone	BuSpar	18 and older
chlordiazepoxide	Librium	18 and older
clonazepam	Klonopin	18 and older
clorazepate	Tranxene	18 and older
diazepam	Valium	18 and older
lorazepam	Ativan	18 and older
oxazepam (generic only)	oxazepam	18 and older

Generic Name	Trade Name	FDA Approved Age

ADHD Medications

(All of these ADHD medications are stimulants, except atomoxetine and guanfacine.)

Generic Name	Trade Name	FDA Approved Age
amphetamine	Adderall	3 and older
amphetamine (extended release)	Adderall XR	6 and older
atomoxetine	Strattera	6 and older
dexmethylphenidate	Focalin	6 and older
dexmethylphenidate (extended release)	Focalin XR	6 and older
dextroamphetamine	Dexedrine, Dextrostat	3 and older
guanfacine	Intuniv	6 and older
lisdexamfetamine dimesylate	Vyvanse	6 and older
methamphetamine	Desoxyn	6 and older
methylphenidate	Ritalin	6 and older
methylphenidate (extended release)	Metadate CD, Metadate ER, Ritalin SR	6 and older
methylphenidate (long-acting)	Ritalin LA, Concerta	6 and older
methylphenidate patch	Daytrana	6 and older
methylphenidate (oral solution and chewable tablets)	Methylin	6 and older

Citations

1. Lieberman JA, Stroup TS, McEvoy JP, Swartz MS, Rosenheck RA, Perkins DO, Keefe RS, Davis SM, Davis CE, Lebowitz BD, Severe J, Hsiao JK; Clinical Antipsychotic Trials of Intervention Effectiveness (CATIE). Effectiveness of antipsychotic drugs in patients with chronic schizophrenia. *New England Journal of Medicine.* 2005 Sep 22;353(12):1209-1223.

2. Rush JA, Trivedi MH, Wisniewski SR, Stewart JW, Nierenberg AA, Thase ME, Ritz L, Biggs MM, Warden D, Luther JF, Shores-Wilson K, Niederehe G, Fava M. Bupropion-SR, sertraline, or venlafaxine-XR after failure of SSRIs for depression. *New England Journal of Medicine.* 2006 Mar 23; 354(12):1231-1242.

3. Trivedi MH, Fava M, Wisniewski SR, Thase ME, Quitkin F, Warden D, Ritz L, Nierenberg AA, Lebowitz BD, Biggs MM, Luther JF, Shores-Wilson K, Rush JA. Medication augmentation after the failure of SSRIs for depression. *New England Journal of Medicine.* 2006 Mar 23; 354(12): 1243-1252.

4. Hypericum Depression Trial Study Group. Effect of Hypericum perforatum (St. John's wort) in major depressive disorder: a randomized controlled trial. *Journal of the American Medical Association.* 2002; 287(14): 1807-1814.

5. Bridge JA, Iyengar S, Salary CB, Barbe RP, Birmaher B, Pincus HA, Ren L, Brent DA. Clinical response and risk for reported suicidal ideation and suicide attempts in pediatric antidepressant treatment, a meta-analysis of randomized controlled trials. *Journal of the American Medical Association.* 2007; 297(15): 1683-1696.

6. Bowden CL, Calabrese JR, McElroy SL, Gyulai L, Wassef A, Petty F, Pope HG, Jr., Chou JC, Keck PE, Jr., Rhodes LJ, Swann AC, Hirschfeld RM, Wozniak PJ, Group DMS. A randomized, placebo-controlled 12-month trial of divalproex and lithium in treatment of outpatients with bipolar I disorder. *Archives of General Psychiatry.* 2000 May; 57(5):481-489.

7. Rothschild AJ, Bates KS, Boehringer KL, Syed A. Olanzapine response in psychotic depression. *Journal of Clinical Psychiatry.* 1999 Feb; 60(2):116-118.

8. Suppes T, Webb A, Paul B, Carmody T, Kraemer H, Rush AJ. Clinical outcome in a randomized 1-year trial of clozapine versus treatment as usual for patients with treatment-resistant illness and a history of mania. *American Journal of Psychiatry.* 1999 Aug;156(8): 1164-1169.

9. Thase ME, Sachs GS. Bipolar depression: pharmacotherapy and related therapeutic strategies. *Biological Psychiatry.* 2000 Sep 15;48(6):558-572.

10. Sachs G, Nierenberg AA, Calabrese JR, Marangell LB, Wisniewski SR, Gyulai L, Friedman ES, Bowden CL, Fossey MD, Ostacher MJ, Ketter TA, Patel J, Hauser P, Rapport D, Martinez JM, Allen MH, Miklowitz DJ, Otto MW, Dennehy EB, Thase ME. Effectiveness of adjunctive antidepressant treatment for bipolar depression: a double-blind placebo-controlled study. *New England Journal of Medicine.* Epub 28 Mar 2007; 356(17): 1771-1773.

11. Vainionpaa LK, Rattya J, Knip M, Tapanainen JS, Pakarinen AJ, Lanning P, Tekay A, Myllyla VV, Isojarvi JI. Valproate-induced hyperandrogenism during pubertal maturation in girls with epilepsy. *Annals of Neurology.* 1999 Apr;45(4):444-450.

12. Joffe H, Cohen LS, Suppes T, McLaughlin WL, Lavori P, Adams JM, Hwang CH, Hall JE, Sachs GS. Valproate is associated with new-onset oligoamenorrhea with hyperandrogenism in women with bipolar disorder. *Biological Psychiatry.* 2006 Jun 1;59(11):1078-1086.

13. Joffe H, Cohen LS, Suppes T, Hwang CH, Molay F, Adams JM, Sachs GS, Hall JE. Longitudinal follow-up of reproductive and metabolic features of valproate-associated polycystic ovarian syndrome features: A preliminary report. *Biological Psychiatry.* 2006 Dec 15;60(12):1378-1381.

14. Wilens TC, Faraone, SV, Biederman J, Gunawardene S. Does stimulant therapy of attention-deficit/hyperactivity disorder beget later substance abuse? A meta-analytic review of the literature. *Pediatrics.* 2003; 111(1):179-185.

15. Swanson J, Greenhill L, Wigal T, Kollins S, Stehli A, Davies M, Chuang S, Vitiello B, Skroballa A, Posner K, Abikoff H, Oatis M, McCracken J, McGough J, Riddle M, Ghouman J, Cunningham C, Wigal S. Stimulant-related reductions in growth rates in the PATS. *Journal of the Academy of Child and Adolescent Psychiatry.* 2006 Nov; 45(11): 1304-1313.

16. Greenhill L, Kollins S, Abikoff H, McCracken J, Riddle M, Swanson J, McGough J, Wigal S, Wigal T, Vitiello B, Skroballa A, Posner K, Ghuman J, Cunningham C, Davies M, Chuang S, Cooper T. Efficacy and safety of immediate-release methylphenidate treatment for preschoolers with attention-deficit/hyperactivity disorder. *Journal of the Academy of Child and Adolescent Psychiatry.* 2006 Nov; 45(11):1284-1293.

17. Wigal T, Greenhill L, Chuang S, McGough J, Vitiello B, Skrobala A, Swanson J, Wigal S, Abikoff H, Kollins S, McCracken J, Riddle M, Posner K, Ghuman J, Davies M, Thorp B, Stehli A. Safety and tolerability of methylphenidate in preschool children with attention-deficit/hyperactivity disorder. *Journal of the Academy of Child and Adolescent Psychiatry*. 2006 Nov; 45(11): 1294-1303.

18. Alwan S, Reefhuis J, Rasmussen S, Olney R, Friedman J for the National Birth Defects Prevention Study. Use of selective serotonin-reuptake inhibitors in pregnancy and the risk of birth defects. *New England Journal of Medicine*. 2007 Jun 28; 356(26):2684-2692.

19. Louik C, Lin An, Werler M, Hernandez S, Mitchell A. First-trimester use of selective serotonin-reuptake inhibitors and the risk of birth defects. *New England Journal of Medicine*. 2007 Jun 28; 356(26):2675-2683.

20. Austin M. To treat or not to treat: maternal depression, SSRI use in pregnancy and adverse neonatal effects. *Psychological Medicine*. 2006 Jul 25; 1-8.

21. Cohen L, Altshuler L, Harlow B, Nonacs R, Newport DJ, Viguera A, Suri R, Burt V, Hendrick AM, Loughead A, Vitonis AF, Stowe Z. Relapse of major depression during pregnancy in women who maintain or discontinue antidepressant treatment. *Journal of the American Medical Association*. 2006 Feb 1; 295(5): 499-507.

22. U.S. Food and Drug Administration (FDA). FDA Medwatch drug alert on Effexor and SSRIs, 2004 Jun 3. Available at www.fda.gov/medwatch/safety/2004/safety04.htm#effexor.

23. Jain AE, Lacy T. Psychotropic drugs in pregnancy and lactation. *Journal of Psychiatric Practice*. 2005 May; 11(3): 177-191.

24. Ward RK, Zamorski MA. Benefits and risks of psychiatric medications during pregnancy. *American Family Physician*. 15 Aug. 2002; 66(4): 629-636.

For More Information on Medications:

Visit the National Library of Medicine's MedlinePlus

http://www.nlm.nih.gov/medlineplus

En Español

http://medlineplus.gov/spanish

For information on Clinical Trials

http://www.nimh.nih.gov/trials/index.shtml

National Library of Medicine Clinical Trials Database

http://www.clinicaltrials.gov

Information from NIMH is available in multiple formats. You can browse online, download documents in PDF, and order paper brochures through the mail. If you would like to have NIMH publications, you can order them online at http://www.nimh.nih.gov. If you do not have Internet access and wish to have information that supplements this publication, please contact the NIMH Information Resource Center at the numbers listed below.

National Institute of Mental Health
Science Writing, Press & Dissemination Branch
6001 Executive Boulevard
Room 8184, MSC 9663
Bethesda, MD 20892-9663
Phone: 301-443-4513 or
1-866-615-NIMH (6464) toll-free
TTY: 301-443-8431 or
        866-415-8051 toll-free
FAX: 301-443-4279
E-mail: **nimhinfo@nih.gov**
Website: **http://www.nimh.nih.gov**

Reprints

NIMH publications are in the public domain and may be reproduced or copied without the permission from the National Institute of Mental Health. NIMH encourages you to reproduce them and use them in your efforts to improve public health. Citation of the National Institute of Mental Health as a source is appreciated. However, using government materials inappropriately can raise legal or ethical concerns, so we ask you to use these guidelines:

- NIMH does not endorse or recommend any commercial products, processes, or services, and publications may not be used for advertising or endorsement purposes.

- NIMH does not provide specific medical advice or treatment recommendations or referrals; these materials may not be used in a manner that has the appearance of such information.

- NIMH requests that non-Federal organizations not alter publications in a way that will jeopardize the integrity and "brand" when using publications.

- Addition of non-Federal Government logos and Web site links may not have the appearance of NIMH endorsement of any specific commercial products or services or medical treatments or services.

- Images used in publications are of models and are used for illustrative purposes only. Use of some images is restricted.

If you have questions regarding these guidelines and use of NIMH publications, please contact the NIMH Information Resource Center at 1-866-615-6464 or e-mail **nimhinfo@nih.gov**.